Discovering Our Nation's Heritage

The Story of

THE PLEDGE OF ALLEGIANCE

JOHN HUDSON TINER

First Printing: March 2003

Copyright © 2003 by New Leaf Press, Inc.
All rights reserved, no part of this book
may be used or reproduced in any manner whatsoever
without written permission of the publisher, except in
the case of brief quotations in articles and reviews. For
information write: New Leaf Press, Inc.
P.O. Box 726
Green Forest, AR 72638

Cover and interior design by Bryan Miller
Photo credits: Library of Congress: 11, 14, 15, 17,
22, 23, 27
ISBN: 0-89051-393-7
Library of Congress Number: 2002116470

Printed in the United States of America

Please visit our website for other great titles

www.newleafpress.net

Master
Books

Table of Contents

The Story of the Pledge of Allegiance

Most

schools today fly a United States flag

outside the building on a flagpole.

In many schools, students start the

day by facing a flag in the classroom

and reciting the Pledge of Allegiance.

However, 125 years ago this was not

true. Only a few school buildings had a flagpole, and most classrooms did not display a United States flag. Students did not say the Pledge of Allegiance because it was not written until 1892.

The meaning of the Pledge of Allegiance and how it came to be written is an exciting story.

Under God

Events that shaped our country also changed the wording of the pledge itself. The most recent change to the pledge occurred in the 1950s. The United States led the free world in rebuilding Europe after the destruction of World War II (1939–1945). The United States believed in freedom, justice, and equality. In the countries that followed the lead of the United States, people could worship God freely. Citizens could work hard and keep what they earned. Democratic countries quickly recovered from the destruction of war.

      Leaders of the Soviet Union also had a plan for rebuilding Europe. Their idea was vastly different from the

American plan. Communist dictators controlled the Soviet Union. They carefully controlled every part of their citizens' lives. They denied people religious freedom and banned Bibles.

People in communist countries longed for liberty and justice as described in the American Pledge of Allegiance. Families forbidden to worship God escaped from communism and streamed into free countries. Communist dictators built fences and walls along their borders to keep people from fleeing their rule.

President Dwight David Eisenhower of the United States led the free world in the 1950s. He believed that Americans should remember the freedoms they enjoyed. God had blessed America because its citizens trusted and served Him.

In the 1950s, Christians asked for the words "under God" to be added to the Pledge of Allegiance. President

Eisenhower agreed. He said, "In this way we shall constantly strengthen those spiritual weapons which forever will be our country's most powerful resource in peace and war."

On June 14, 1954, Flag Day, President Eisenhower signed the law that added "under God" to the Pledge of Allegiance. He said, "Millions of our schoolchildren will daily proclaim in every city and town, every village and rural schoolhouse, the dedication of our nation and our people to the Almighty."

The Pledge of Allegiance "I pledge allegiance to the flag of the United States of America and to the republic for which it stands, one nation under God, indivisible, with liberty and justice for all."

Flag Day is June 14 each year in the United States. That date is the birthday of the United States flag. On June 14, 1777, the Continental Congress accepted the design of a red, white, and blue flag. Although Flag Day is not a legal holiday, patriotic individuals celebrate the date by flying the American flag.

The United States Flag is also known as Old Glory, the Stars and Stripes, and the Star-Spangled Banner. The 50 stars stand for the 50 states of the Union, and the 13 stripes stand for the original 13 colonies that became the first 13 states.

Dwight David Eisenhower served as President of the United States from 1953 to 1961. During his presidency, "under God" became part of the Pledge of Allegiance and "In God We Trust" became the national motto.

Eisenhower came from the small town of Abilene, Kansas. His family was poor. As a teenager, he worked at a local business to earn money so his older brother could attend college. Later, Eisenhower attended the military academy at West Point. He eventually earned the rank of general. During World War II, General Eisenhower became the commander of the soldiers who defeated the army of Adolph Hitler, the Führer (leader) of Germany.

Because of his honesty and friendly smile, people encouraged Eisenhower to run for president. He easily won the election. As the chief executive of the nation, he offered this prayer: "Give us, we pray, the power to discern clearly right from wrong, and allow all our words and actions to be governed thereby."

My Flag

The 1954 addition of "under God" was not the first change to the Pledge of Allegiance. Another change had occurred in 1923. The words "my flag" in the original pledge were replaced with "the flag of the United States of America." Why the change? The new wording came about because a large number of United States citizens had been born in other countries.

War, disease, famine, and lack of freedom are the main reasons that people leave their homelands and come to America. In 1620, the Pilgrims sailed to the New World seeking a better life and religious freedom. Upon landing in Massachusetts, their leaders wrote the Mayflower Compact. The Mayflower Compact formed a government that was run by the people. The new colony would be ruled by the will of the majority. They agreed to follow just and equal laws. The Mayflower Compact

became the first American freedom document.

Over the years, the opportunities offered by America attracted other settlers. In the 1840s, Ireland suffered a terrible famine. The potato crop, their staple food, failed. More than a million people died. Of those who survived, many made their way to the United States. At the same time, Hispanics came to America from Mexico, Central America, South America, and Caribbean islands such as Cuba and Puerto Rico.

During the 1850s and 1860s, Chinese from Asia immigrated to San Francisco and other large cities along the West Coast. Chinese laborers worked hard to help build the first transcontinental railroad. The completion of the railroad in

1869 made travel across America much easier. Trains opened the vast interior of the nation to settlement.

Coming to America was an attractive idea to people from Europe. They saw that in America, poor people had unlimited possibilities. The Bill of Rights guaranteed basic freedoms for everyone, including the poor. Abraham Lincoln had been born in poverty in a log cabin, yet he had risen to become president of the nation.

How could poor people afford to cross the ocean by steamship, pay for a train ticket to the Midwest, and then buy land? Yet, determined people found a way. They offered to work for American companies that would pay for their steamship tickets. Immigrants promised to work for a certain period, usually four years.

Other immigrants saved enough money to come over. Ships offered cheap tickets for poor immigrants. The trip was uncomfortable and passengers were packed aboard. A one-way ticket from England to New York was only about 32 dollars. The train fare from New York to Chicago was 14 dollars. At that time a worker made about 7 dollars a month. Land east of the Mississippi River could be bought for 2 dollars an acre. Land west of the Mississippi River was free. After establishing a home in America, an immigrant could earn enough in

two years to send for other members of his family.

In 1890, the population of the United States was 63 million. By 1920, it had risen to 100 million. More than half of the population gain was immigrant — about 20 million people. Eventually, the United States would become the third most populous country in the world. Only China and India would have more people.

The United States became known as a "melting pot" because its people came from so many different countries.

At that time, the Pledge of Allegiance began with "I pledge allegiance to my flag." When immigrants said the Pledge of Allegiance, did they understand what the words "my flag" meant? Was it the flag of the country where they were born?

The National Flag Conference addressed the question in 1923. Two patriotic groups, the American Legion and the Daughters of the American Revolution conducted the conference. They suggested that the words "the flag of the United States of America" be substituted for "my flag." Their idea was quickly adopted.

The Pledge of Allegiance was originally known as the Salute to the Flag. Children raised their right hands to their foreheads in salute. As they said the pledge, they extended their arms to point toward the flag.

In the 1930s, Adolph Hitler became head of the Nazi party of Germany. People saluted Hitler by bringing their right hands to the middle of their chests and raising it toward the Nazi flag. Nazi law required that people greet one another with the same salute and the words, "Heil, Hitler!"

Hitler became one of the most infamous tyrants in history. The United States declared war against Hitler in 1941. Americans objected to the salute because raising the hand toward the flag looked like a Nazi salute. Instead, they said the pledge with their right hands over their hearts. The United States Congress agreed to the change in 1942. Congress also changed the name from the Salute to the Flag to the Pledge of Allegiance.

For most immigrants, the port of entry was New York Harbor. As their ship neared the United States, some stood at the rail to be the first to glimpse the welcome sight of the Statue of Liberty. Others, however, were so eager to begin a new life, they were below deck getting their luggage together. They wanted to be first off the ship.

The First Pledge

On October 12, 1892, a great event occurred in the United States that had never happened before. In schools around the nation, 12 million school children took part in a Columbus Day program. They raised the American flag and for the first time said the Pledge of Allegiance.

Great events do not happen by chance. People with vision and leadership are needed. Three dedicated individuals brought the Pledge of Allegiance to the nation. One was Daniel Ford, a magazine publisher. The other two were his employees, James Upham and Francis Bellamy.

Daniel Ford published a magazine named *The Youth's Companion*. His goal was to make the magazine interesting to both children and parents. He chose a mix of short stories, articles about science and current events, poetry, and puzzles.

For the fiction, he selected stories filled with action and adventure. Writers included Mark Twain and Bret Harte. For non-fiction, he printed articles by individuals that he admired such as Presidents Grover Cleveland and John Quincy Adams. He published poetry by Emily Dickinson.

Ford wanted *The Youth's Companion* to be a positive religious force. He believed in Jesus and sought to direct the content of his magazine by Christian principles.

Under Daniel Ford's leadership, *The Youth's Companion* quickly became the largest circulation weekly magazine in the nation. About one-half million people subscribed to it. The magazine had something for every member of the family.

Daniel Ford also hired people of exceptional skill to work for the magazine. One of those individuals was James Upham, his nephew.

James Upham realized that success of the magazine depended on an educated population. Activities that increased school attendance and helped students learn to read would benefit the magazine. He worked with teachers to print information in the magazine for use in their classrooms.

Most rural children attended school in a one-room building. One teacher taught all of the students. The buildings were plain, poorly furnished, and often unheated. The schoolyards were bare earth with a few blades of grass beaten flat by the countless footsteps of school children.

Upham began a program to improve country schoolhouses. In *The Youth's Companion,* he published plans for planting trees and shrubs. He printed nature guides so children would recognize and appreciate native plants and animals.

Many children were immigrants. Upham believed they needed a firmer grounding in patriotic ideas. He was disappointed that only military bases flew United States flags. Most schools had neither a flagpole nor a flag.

In 1888, James Upham offered to sell a large, good quality flag for ten dollars. However, in the 1880s, that was a lot of money. School districts were hard pressed to buy schoolbooks and pay teachers their salaries of about 25 dollars per month. Buying a flag for every building was beyond their means.

To solve this problem, Upham called for volunteer schoolchildren to raise money to purchase flags for their school. He sent each volunteer 100 cards. The volunteer sold the cards for ten cents each. The student who bought the card received 1/100th of a share in the flag. School children saved their pennies to buy cards. By selling 100 cards, the volunteer raised ten dollars for the flag. School districts found poles for the flag. In all, school children of America bought about

30,000 flags. For the first time, American schools had the Stars and Stripes outside.

Upham was also surprised to learn that children of immigrant families often did not know the names of America's heroes. He had his magazine print portraits of famous Americans. Pictures of George Washington

and Abraham Lincoln decorated the walls of American classrooms. He offered illustrations of important events such as a painting called "Spirit of '76." It showed a scene from the Revolutionary War (1775–1783). He also offered an exciting drawing of Christopher Columbus landing in the New World.

The great Italian navigator Christopher Columbus was one of the most famous persons in history. Millions of immigrants in the United States did not know the American presidents, but they had heard of Christopher Columbus.

The United States planned a large celebration for October 12, 1892. Four hundred years earlier, Columbus had opened America to settlement. President Benjamin Harrison declared October 12 a national holiday. Congress passed a resolution for a celebration, known as the Columbian Exposition; a world's fair, to be held in Chicago.

James Upham knew that most people would not be able to go to the fair, especially poor children. He decided that every school across the nation should do something special on Columbus Day. Everyone could take part in the celebration, even those unable to attend the World's Fair. He wrote a

program centered on raising a school flag. The World's Fair committee agreed that the Upham's school program would be part of the official celebration.

Slowly the flag-raising program took shape. At each school, a message from President Harrison would be read: "Let the National Flag float over every school house in the country and impress upon our youth the patriotic duties of American citizenship." The children would salute as veterans raised the flag.

Upham believed that God had given the United States a divine mission to show the world how to live right. The assembly would acknowledge God with a prayer and a reading from the Bible. Students would sing "America" ("My Country 'tis of Thee"). A speaker would then tell about important events in the history of the United States.

As Upham looked at the program, he wanted the children to have a greater role. Rather than merely saluting the flag, he decided the children should recite a patriotic statement. He tried to write a salute to the flag. It gave him a lot of trouble. He wanted words that would tell why the United States was worthy of allegiance.

James Upham tried many different salutes and read them to Daniel Ford and others. Neither he nor anyone else was satisfied.

The Youth's Companion with the Columbus Day program would be mailed to readers on September 8, 1892. As the deadline approached, Upham grew more desperate for a salute to the flag. He asked Francis Bellamy for help.

Francis Bellamy was Daniel Ford's assistant. Francis Bellamy had been a preacher at the Dearborn Street Church in Boston. Daniel Ford attended that church and heard Bellamy's sermons. Bellamy spoke about liberty and patriotism, and how the love of Jesus applied to all people. The sermons impressed Ford. He asked Bellamy to join the staff of *The Youth's Companion.*

Bellamy began working on a salute to the flag in August. He had definite ideas about it. The pledge should emphasize the American ideas of liberty and justice. All people enjoyed those benefits. In addition, he believed everyone should work together — that the United States was one nation.

Like Upham, Bellamy found it difficult to write a short pledge. Late in August, 1892, he gave his result to Upham for approval.

James Upham read the pledge, quickly memorized the words, and then spoke aloud the Salute to the Flag for the first time: "I pledge allegiance to my flag and to the republic for which it stands: one nation indivisible, with liberty and justice for all."

The pledge and Columbus Day program were published in *The Youth's Companion* on September 8, 1892. Leaflets with the same information were sent to schools throughout the country. The big day arrived on October 12, 1892. Twelve million students in every state in the nation said the Pledge of Allegiance.

In an age before radio or television, the family would gather around to listen to popular magazines being read aloud. When the family finished the magazine, they often passed it to neighbors who did not subscribe. The total number of people who

read a magazine such as *The Youth's Companion* was often far greater than the number of copies printed.

James Upham found a salute to the flag that had been used in New York City. That salute said, "We give our heads and our hearts to God and our country; one country; one language; one flag." He did not use this one because it did not tell why a person should pledge allegiance to the United States.

Neither Francis Bellamy's nor James Upham's names appeared as authors of the pledge or Columbus Day program. Daniel Ford believed that his magazine was a team effort. Authors did not sign their names to material in the magazine. For that reason, it was not clear who had actually written the pledge. Some said Upham but others gave the honor to Bellamy. Not until 1939 did an investigation show that Francis Bellamy wrote the pledge. However, James Upham had the idea for a pledge. Without his leadership and the support of Daniel Ford, the pledge would never have been accepted.

Gilbert Stuart (1755-1828). His painting of Washington, in which the lower part is unfinished, became the most popular of his portraits. It was published by *The Youth's Companion* and sent to schools throughout America. Some of these original prints from the magazine can still be seen in historic buildings.

The "Spirit of '76" is a heroic painting showing events during the Revolutionary War. Archibald MacNeal Willard (1836-1918) painted it to celebrate the 100th anniversary of the Declaration

of Independence. His grandfather had fought in the Revolutionary War. His father was a preacher who served as the model for the central figure.

James Upham urged school volunteers to form a group called "Mending the Flag." He prepared a kit with red, white and blue cloth, needles, thread and scissors. The kit was sent free for two new subscribers to *The Youth's Companion*. Students, mostly girls, used the kit to keep the United States flag in good repair.

Christopher Columbus

(1451-1506) was an Italian navigator who sailed for Spain. He boldly suggested that India could be reached by sailing in the opposite direction — west rather than east. He sailed with three small ships: Santa Maria, Nina, and Pinta. October 12, 1492, Columbus stepped ashore on a small island. He fell to his knees, kissed the earth and gave thanks to God. He named the island

San Salvador, which means "the Savior." Despite earlier voyages by the Vikings, Columbus is honored as the one who discovered America. The native Americans did not know that Europe existed, and the Europeans did not know about the New World. Columbus discovered America because he made each group aware that the other existed.

What the Pledge Means

The Pledge of Allegiance is short. When first written, it had only 23 words. Today, it has 31 words. A person can recite it in less than ten seconds. The pledge could lose its meaning when repeated often. However, by thinking about the words, the importance of the pledge becomes clear and its meaning fresh.

A "pledge" is an earnest promise. By saying the Pledge of Allegiance, a person promises to be loyal to the United States, support the Constitution, and obey the nation's laws. "Allegiance" means to give faithful service even in the face of hardships. At the start of the American Revolutionary War (1775–1783), Thomas Paine wrote,

hese are times that try men's souls. The summer soldier and the
nshine patriot will in this crisis shrink from the service of their
untry." But a person who pledges allegiance must give steadfast
pport despite difficult times.

The "flag" is a symbol. The United States flag stands for
erything that is good about the United States. People can worship
od and express their opinions freely. They can meet with friends
d be safe in their homes. If charged with crimes, they are judged
rly. To enjoy these freedoms, a person must accept the duties of
zenship. One duty is to be loyal to the United States and put it
ead of other countries.

The "United States of America" is one country made of 50

states all united with a common purpose and under the same federal laws.

The United States is a "republic." We vote for our leaders. When the United States came into existence, people in other countries had little to say about who would rule them. Kings came into power because they were members of nobility, or military leaders took over the government by force. In the United States, the change of leadership comes without fighting. The United States is a democracy, a Greek word that means "the people rule." Change comes by ballot box and not battlefield.

The United States is "one nation." Can a state leave the Union and become a separate nation? Can the United States be divided into smaller nations? This question was answered during the Civil War (1861–1865).

When Abraham Lincoln took office as president, the United States had 33 states. Following Lincoln's election, 11 southern states separated from the United States and formed a new nation. They called themselves the Confederate States of America. People in the 22 remaining states believed that the southern states had to remain in the Union. Northern states wanted to free the four million black slaves that worked in the South.

A terrible Civil War began between the United States of America (the Union, or North) and the Confederate States of America (the Confederacy, or South). More than 600,000 soldiers died. In the end, slaves were freed and southern states returned to the Union.

The word "indivisible" in the pledge refers to the fact that the United States cannot be broken into smaller countries. Since the Civil War, the United States has become the strongest nation in the world. One of the reasons is because all of the states act as one country.

The words "under God" reflect the thinking of Thomas Jefferson and other founders of the United States. They believed God, and not government, was the source of freedom. In the Declaration of Independence, Jefferson stated that "all men are created equal; that they are endowed by their Creator with certain unalienable rights; that

among these are life, liberty, and the pursuit of happiness." God, not governments, gives liberty.

Abraham Lincoln used the phrase "under God" in his famous speech at Gettysburg Battlefield on November 19, 1863. Near the end of his short speech, Lincoln said, "This nation, under God, shall have a new birth of freedom."

"Liberty" is one of the most important ideas in the Constitution. The first paragraph of the Constitution says that the United States was established to secure the blessings of liberty. Liberty means freedom — the right to act, believe, or express yourself as you choose. The word "justice" means fair treatment. The last two words of the Pledge of Allegiance are "for all." Everyone in the country is entitled to enjoy the benefits of living in America.

Lincoln's Gettysburg Address. On November 19, 1863, Lincoln traveled by train to Gettysburg, Pennsylvania, to attend the dedication of a national cemetery. The event remembered the soldiers — both North and South — who died during a fierce battle that lasted three days, July 1-3, 1863. Edward Everett, a well-known orator, gave the main speech. He spoke for two hours. Abraham Lincoln's speech lasted for only two minutes. Known as Lincoln's Gettysburg Address, it is the most famous speech ever given by an American.

A constitution contains laws that govern a country. The Constitution of the United States is the oldest one still in use. Many other countries have modeled their constitutions after ours.

James Upham's program for schools on Columbus Day included singing the song "America." The song described America as a "Sweet land of liberty." The last line says, "Protect us by Thy might, Great God, our King!"

Pledge of Allegiance Today

Freedom

of speech is guaranteed by the Constitution of the United States. A person also has the freedom not to speak. In 1943, the United States Supreme Court said that students could not be forced to say the Pledge of Allegiance. However, the vast majority of people, both children and adults, are pleased to show their dedication to the ideals of the United States by reciting the Pledge of Allegiance.

The phrase "under God" in the pledge has also been questioned. However, the Supreme Court itself begins each session with the phrase "God save the United States and this honorable court." Federal officials recite an oath [pledge] of office that ends with the statement "so help me God."

Statements calling upon the help and blessing of God are found in many of the songs sung at public events. These songs include "God Bless America" and "America the

Beautiful." The national motto of the United States is "In God We Trust."

The founders of the United States realized that the Constitution and laws passed by Congress could only go so far in making a great nation. John Adams, who was the second president of the United States, said, "Our Constitution was designed only for a moral and religious people." John Adams understood that each person had to do his or her part by being honest and doing right.

More than 100 years have passed since 12 million school children said the Pledge of Allegiance for the first time in 1892. Today, more than half of the states set aside time for students to say the Pledge of Allegiance. The pledge has continued to be recited daily by children in schools across America.

After immigrants learn their duties and responsibilities, they can become citizens of the United States. The final step is to take the oath of allegiance. In part, they say, "I hereby declare ... that I will support and defend the Constitution and laws of the United States of America against all enemies, foreign and domestic ... so help me God."

Displaying the Flag. The flag is raised briskly but lowered slowly and with ceremony. Normally it is flown only in good weather from sunrise to sunset. It can

be flown at night if lighted. The flag should never touch anything beneath it. It should never be used as wearing apparel. But a flag patch can be sewn to the uniforms of military personnel, firemen, policemen, and emergency workers. The flag can be printed on paper, but not if the paper is to be used for some other purpose and discarded. The accepted method to dispose of a tattered flag is by burning.

The colors of the United States Flag have special meaning. Red is for courage, white for purity, and blue for loyalty.

Freedom Statements

(see activity 3)

From the Declaration of Independence: We hold these truths to be self-evident, that all men are created equal, that they are endowed by their Creator with certain unalienable rights, that among these are life, liberty and the pursuit of happiness. That to secure these rights, governments are instituted among men, deriving their just powers from the consent of the governed.

The preamble to the Constitution: We the people of the United States, in order to form a more perfect Union, establish justice, insure domestic tranquility, provide for the common defense, promote the general welfare, and secure the blessings of liberty to ourselves and our posterity, do ordain and establish the Constitution for the United States of America.

Bill of Rights, Article I: Congress shall make no law respecting an establishment of religion, or prohibiting the free exercise thereof; or abridging the freedom of speech, or of the press; or the right of the people peaceably to assemble, and to petition the government for a redress of grievances.

The first paragraph of Lincoln's Gettysburg Address: Fourscore and seven years ago our fathers brought forth upon this continent a new nation, conceived in liberty, and dedicated to the proposition that all men are created equal.

Questions

A B C D The Pledge of Allegiance was written (A. at the
founding of Jamestown Colony, 1607   B. at the signing of the
Declaration of Independence, 1776   C. for a Columbus Day
celebration, 1892   D. at the start of World War II, 1941).

T F The phrase "under God" was not in the original Pledge of
Allegiance.

A B The Pilgrims came to the New World seeking a better life
and (A. gold   B. religious freedom).

A B C D America's first freedom document was (A. the Bill
of Rights   B. the Constitution   C. the Declaration of
Independence   D. the Mayflower Compact).

The United States became known as a _____ pot
because its people were from so many different countries.

A B C D The words "my flag" in the original Pledge of
Allegiance were changed to (A. my banner   B. my flag
and my country   C. the American flag   D. the flag of the
United States of America).

A B C D The only countries with more people than the United
States are China and (A. India   B. Ireland   C. Mexico
D. Russia).

A B C D The historical person that immigrants knew best was

43

(A. Abraham Lincoln   B. Benjamin Franklin

C. Christopher Columbus   D. George Washington).

T F A pledge is a promise.

In Lincoln's Gettysburg Address, he said that America was

conceived in _____.

A B C D The national motto of the United States is (A. God

Smiled on Our Country   B. In God We Trust   C. Liberty

and Justice for All   D. One Nation, Under God).

A B C D John Adams said, "Our Constitution was designed

only for (A. a country separated from religion   B. a moral

and hard-working people   C. a moral and religious people

D. a nation founded on competition).

Answers to Questions

C for a Columbus Day celebration, 1892

T

B religious freedom

D the Mayflower Compact

melting

D the Flag of the United States of America.

A India

C Christopher Columbus

T

liberty

B In God We Trust

C a moral and religious people

Activities

1. How many flags can you count on your route to school? Are there other flags on the same pole with the United States flag? Does your school have a flagpole outside? Does your classroom have a flag? Why is a United States flag sometimes flown at half staff (lowered halfway down the flagpole)?

2. Does your school have a set time for students to recite the Pledge of Allegiance to the flag? How often? Do you sometimes have an outside flag-raising ceremony?

3. Memorize one of the freedom statements given in the Freedom Statements sidebar.

4. Draw a poster with the words of the Pledge of Allegiance on it. Decorate the poster with symbols of the nation such as the American bald eagle, Statue of Liberty, and American flag.

5. Write a poem or short essay that expresses why you want the United States to be "under God."

6. Chose one of the following Americans, select one of their

characteristics that you admire, and write a short paragraph explaining why you think what they did was important.

John Quincy Adams

Grover Cleveland

Christopher Columbus

Emily Dickinson

Dwight David Eisenhower

Thomas Jefferson

Abraham Lincoln

Mark Twain (Samuel Clemens)

George Washington

7. If you could add anything to the Pledge of Allegiance, what would you add? Write the pledge with your new words and say it aloud.

Glossary

American Legion is an organization of former members of the United States military.

Bill of Rights is made of the first ten amendments to the U.S. Constitution to protect our rights.

Circulation is the number of copies of a magazine that are sold.

A **civil war** is a conflict between citizens of the same country. The American Civil War was fought between the northern states and southern states.

Continental Congress was a group of representatives from each state that approved the Declaration of Independence and Constitution.

Daughters of the American Revolution is a patriotic association of women who are direct descendents of soldiers or others who fought for American independence.

Deadline is the time limit for the completion of an assignment.

The **federal government** is the main government of the United States. Under it are state, county, city, and other local governments.

Hispanics are people from the countries south of the United States that speak Spanish. These countries include Mexico, parts of Central America, South America, and some island nations in the Caribbean.

Ideals are honorable or worthy goals.

A legal holiday is one in which government business is halted to commemorate a special event.

Nobility is a class of people who inherit rank because of their birth rather than achievement; kings and queens are members of nobility.

A preamble is the first paragraph or introduction to a formal document.

Staple food is the food that provides the largest amount of food energy for a country. About half of the world depends on rice as their principle staple food. Other staple foods include wheat, potatoes, and corn.

Union Union is a term emphasize that the United States is one nation.

Veterans are people who served their country in the military.